Poems
For Ukraine

By Judy Sevec

Rapier
PUBLISHING COMPANY

Poems for Ukraine

ISBN 978-1-946683-48-9
Library of Congress Control Number 2022912257

Rapier Publishing Company
Dothan, Alabama 36301

www.rapierpublishing.com
Facebook: www.rapierpublishing@gmail.com
Twitter: rapierpublishing@rapierpub

Printed in the United States of America

Book Cover Design: Daniel Ojedokum
Book Layout: Rapture Graphics
Shutterstock Photos/ Enhanced Licenses
#602821022/ #1166262265

Dedication

I dedicate this book to the People of Ukraine.

Love Judy Sevec

WORDS FROM THE AUTHOR

When I first saw Russia's War against
Ukraine on the news, it was so bad!
Well, it got worse, and even more cruel and horrendous.
It broke my heart for the people of Ukraine.
They deeply impressed me with how patriotic
and brave they are.

It upset me. I tried to stop watching the news and
just pray for them, but I kept watching the news.
I wanted to know what was happening.

They interviewed a beautiful young woman with a child.
She was very charismatic, and very vulnerable.
They interviewed her several times.
She had a little girl and a baby boy.
They had to flee to keep them safe while the dad,
her husband, had to stay and fight.
It touched my heart and soul.

God put it on my heart to write this book of poems
and donate 50% of profits to help the people of Ukraine.

Thank you, Judy Sevec

POEMS FOR UKRAINE

UKRAINE

A beautiful country with beautiful people
Big, Big cities
Fields of golden wheat
Old ancient churches with golden steeples
Ukrainian people are lovely and inspiring and brave
They only long to stay free
Never a slave to be
To stay friends with all,
All who pray for them
And love these dear people
Who God meant to be free!

LIFT THEM UP IN PRAYER

Dear God, we pray for these people, so brave
People I know that you can save
Let the whole world lift them up in prayer
Their unity and resolve so rare
Let them know that the world does care

DON'T EVER LOOK AWAY

Let the whole world pray for Ukraine
Put money in the collection plate
Wear yellow and blue
Attend a protest or two
Always pray what can we do
How can the world see in real time
What's going on and only sanctions and talk?
Don't just look away
Don't balk
But whole world open every church door
and have a special service
Meet at the town square and all lift up prayers
for the people of Ukraine
For God to take away their pain!

SOLDIERS

They are a ragged bunch of soldiers,
but they have heart
They've fought for freedom from the start
Mother Mary is on their side, 'cause they were so outnum-
bered, but kept up the fight
So many people praying they make it through
another night
And live to see the light…
And live to see the Light…

FREEDOM AND PEACE

I always did like yellow and especially blue
And now they'll always make me think of you
Your country was so vibrant and alive
But now, I think when will more help arrive
I will keep you in my prayers every day
From now on, I'll think of Ukraine's people
and how in their homes they want to stay
And to have the war cease
Just to stay and live in freedom and peace

PRAY

And then I looked and then I saw
How could this be?
I couldn't believe what I saw
Everyone said, "Never Again."
But now – here it is Again!
It's WAR again on innocent people
who never did anything wrong
Just living their lives and moving along
Living their lives and going to and fro where they belong
How could everything go so wrong?
So, march and sing and pray
And pray and pray and pray …

SEEKING HELP

I don't know what to do
It's like the world has gone so wrong
How could it go so astray and not be strong?
Now my world I do not know
I don't even know where to go
The war in Ukraine has upset me so bad
Like so many others, we feel so sad
We want to help and don't know how
We give what we can and pray and seek help
for the people in Ukraine NOW!

HELP

Do you have a TV?
Have you seen?
If you have a TV, you've probably seen
Help! HELP! HELP!
Oh, pray more help for Ukraine
It's just heart-breaking,
You know for real
But you don't know
What to do or feel…
But we all give and pray, pray, pray
Please make this torment go away
Bring to this country a brighter day!

DEMON

I know you heard of angels and devils too
But this turned out to be a demon we never knew
He must be a demon to destroy so many towns
and leave so few
What, oh what can we do?
We want this to come to an end
Then maybe their hearts can mend

THEIR PETS

I see these dear people love their pets
They leave their homes with a suitcase and a cat
Also, I see many flee with their dogs and all that
These people look so precious to me
There's a beautiful girl they show with her baby
Girls and boys with their
Daddy's left behind to fight,
Sometimes they run with their children
and pets in the night
They run and hide across the border to try
and stay safe with their pets and children,
What a sight

WIN

I saw a picture of their cities
They had tall buildings, cafés and meetings
They had lots of apartments
But now they are taking a beating
Big cities and small towns
There are bombs and bombs all around
Shots ring out in the night and still they fight
They're such brave women and men
And they must WIN
They must WIN!

MY HEART

And then before I went to bed
I watched the evening news
I wish I never had
More bad news than good
It really changed my mood
I'd love to go to Poland and hand out food
Or whatever I could do
If I was younger, I would go
I know I would
I wish I could go-
Just to do my part from my heart

COURAGE OF A LION

President Zelensky pleads with the rest
of the world for more help
He begs for tanks and planes
Why does he have to explain?
As the people of the world can see
what's happening on TV
To a land that was free
People of Ukraine are courageous, and they fight
Let's don't let them down
But back them with all of our might!
Countries of the world,
give them more help, PLEASE!

GOD BLESS POLAND

The government and people of Poland
They open up their hearts and homes
To these dear people who felt so alone
When they crossed across their border
They felt safe and secure
They had escaped so much violence and hate
Oh, God, bless Poland for their generous
help to these needy people
Thank you, Poland, for giving them help and hope

CARE

What's wrong with the world?
Do people care?
Talk about the murders in Ukraine
What can we do?
What can we do?
There must be something that we can do
Are our options so few?
Sometimes there's even silence from the world
How can this be- when the horrors we see?
Please stand up, world
Take a stand against evil
Please make a plan

REMEMBER

Remember when the world said, "Never Again?"
Guess they didn't mean it
They said it over and over after the last time
I thought they meant it
No country could ever again cross the line
Never never, not another time
I really believe the world meant it
After World Wars I and II,
I thought they knew!
But here we are again
And our world doesn't care enough
Maybe they care, but…just not enough

BE SO GLAD

At one point I turned off the news
I was so sad
Then I turned it off' cause I was so mad
But if Ukraine won, we'd be so glad!

WHAT TO DO?

I knew I needed to write a poem for Ukraine
But, what else can I do?
Little ol' me – what can I do?
Every day I wear yellow and blue
What a tiny, tiny thing to do
But every night and day,
I pray to God Almighty, 'cause He's the King
He can fix anything!

BLESSED

You know in this country we are so blessed
So many people in other countries
have so much stress
We have stress too,
What should we buy next?
Who should we text?
Where should we go out to eat?
I wonder if my team will get beat
Should I get an electric car?
What time should I go to the local bar?
Will I get a raise at work?
Can I get another perk?
Let's just don't take for granted how blessed we are
Let's give our support to people in need,
Whether near or far!

PEACEFUL PEOPLE

Ukraine, what a beautiful country, beautiful people
Living in peace and harmony
Beautiful snow-covered hills and steeples
They're a peaceful people
Lots of bustling busy cities and towns,
And now it's all turned upside down

IMAGINE

Imagine if you had to leave your home with a suitcase
and a few belongings
What would you take with you?
A few treasured photos and a change of clothing?
What if you knew you may never return…
Your future so uncertain
Can you imagine so many people
are hurting so bad,
Longing for the freedom that they had
Imagine...

OVER

We thought (like Russia did)
it would be over in a week or two,
But this awful war goes on and on
Who thought it would last so long, who knew?
How long since peace reigned in Ukraine?
When will peace return?
When can they rebuild?
When can its people return?
Another war could come and go
When will people learn?

PATRIOTISM

It was at the Russia Ambassador's
townhouse in NYC
They projected Yellow & Blue and the words
"Putin" a war criminal and "Zelensky a Hero"
And then- they gathered and sang
Ukraine's National Anthem!
Such patriotism, Ukraine's people, and supporters,
God Bless Them

RAINBOW

I looked up and saw a rainbow in the sky
And my hopes soared so high
Could this end before too long?
Could things be put back as they belong
I looked up at the rainbow again
Lord, Lord make this end
All these hearts and souls mend
Heal Ukraine, my Lord, so dear,
Please, please come so near
Take away the fears
And wipe away their tears

GO HOME

We must keep the faith
And pray to God
He can fix anything
Don't give up hope
He can fix it all
He's God
He hears us when we call
Right now, the world is in chaos
Now Russia is in Kyiv
But they must leave
Russia, Go Home
Russia, Russia
Please GO HOME!

DEVIL

There's an evil Power-
Hungry man out there
He seems to be the devil – personified
He will kill and destroy
Filled with hate
Someone please stop him…
Before it's too late

CONCERT

Everyone rallied for Ukraine
Bono, U-2, performed "Stand By Me"
with a Ukrainian Pop Star, Tara Topolia,
A singer and soldier, in a bomb shelter.
It was in Kyiv
No one wanted to leave

ON THEIR SIDE

Lord, help there's bombs and bullets everywhere
Everyone ran, but not fast enough
Hanging on to life in Ukraine is tough
They've cried and cried
The people have tried and tried
These people are outnumbered but still they win
Goodness, liberty, and freedom
are on their side until the end

LOVE OF PETS

I wish we could go to help these people
But we have our pets here
I see them as they flee
They love their pets too, but are in such fear
I saw them, bags in one hand,
and kitty in the other
Others had bags and a dog or two
Many in Ukraine- they love their pets, too
What a shame they had to flee
When home is where they yearn to be.

NIGHTMARE

There was a young mother they interviewed on TV
With her little girl and baby boy,
She had to leave to keep them safe,
While their dad stayed behind to fight
Young families torn apart
Like so many others who had to take flight
Some hid in dark basements in the dead of the night
When will this nightmare be over?
Can they ever return?
Can this go away, all this cruelty and strife?
We pray day and night
Lord, give them back their life!

HELP

I say my prayers and go to bed
As I lay my head on my pillow at night
I think of those people over there
Do they even have a pillow, a quilt, or a bed?
Each night do they have a
safe place to lay their head?
And what will they do when the morning comes?
They can't go to work, and they can't go home
They must feel so alone
We're all so proud of Poland for doing her part
For these brave people, they really have a heart

PRAY

I wish this didn't bother me so bad – but it does
And what can I do?
Our church took up a collection
Of course, we gave
But that's not enough
What can we do?
Where's the U.N.?
What can they do?
What could all the countries of the world
get together and do?
What can we say?
But I know that I'll worry and
Pray, Pray, Pray!

WHAT'S THE ANSWER?

You know I feel bad
I had my breakfast,
I had my lunch
I even had my dinner
Then I think of all those people in Ukraine
And I feel so bad
And it makes me feel so sad
I think of the people stuck in Mariupol'
Do they have any food?
Do they have any more water?
Who can they call?
What's the answer, y'all?

COME BACK

What can I do?
What can I say?
The chaos goes on and on
I know the Son will come back soon
I wonder when will He come back
and save His people
From all over the world
Save His people
And end the hurt

BEFORE

How long has this war gone on?
Putin thought he would win in a week
But that was not to be
Now this war has gone on too long
See, Putin thought Ukraine was weak
But the war was wrong
And Ukraine was strong
But what will happen?
I wish we could go back
Back to before all this pain
Back before this war began.

END!

Times are so challenging
So, we must believe
Don't let this be the darkest eve
Don't let this be the eve of the end
There's more help we have to send
Maybe it won't be the end
Maybe all help God will send
He can send help
to make this terrible war end!
Yes, Lord, make it end!

LOVE TREY

We were carefree and we were having fun
Then we turned the TV on
A reporter who touches my heart,
Trey Yingst, was on
He's back in Ukraine
His friend was killed there
I pray he stays safe and well
I know it's like he's back in hell
I was worried about Trey Yingst
But my friend found for me
That he had to take a break and went
back to New York
But now he was drawn back into the dark
I pray he stays safe and can return
To walk again through Central Park
I pray this war will end
And nothing like this will happen again.

OLIGARCHS

Never before have we heard of an Oligarch
Now we hear about Russia's Oligarch everyday
Could this even be a way
A way to make a difference in any way
Could we even touch the influence
of an oligarch's sway?
We know they are rich and powerful
But do they have a soul?
Do they support the war going on?
Do they wish they could bring their boys home?
Or maybe they can't do it alone
Some of the sons of Ukrainians and Russians
are being killed for no purpose
And leaving widows and children alone

ROSARY

Pray the Rosary for Ukraine
Virgin Mary look over their land.
With her strong hand, they will stand.
She'll embrace them,
And in the end, they'll win.

FLAMES

It is an echo of World Wars I and II
Could it become World War III
I hope this is not to be.
It already feels that way to Ukraine
Hitler was EVIL
Putin is TOO.
What, oh what can we do?
Satan must be proud of Putin
'Cause Satan loves
death and destruction
and shooting.
Satan and his minions must be dancing
While war and killing they hasten-
They dance on graves as no one do
they desire to save
But someday they will be defeated
And go down in flames

MARIUPOL

What a beautiful name
I'm sure it was a beautiful place, a beautiful port city
Now I wonder will it ever be the same?
Now the city lays in ruins
What a pity.
Mariupol belongs to Ukraine
what Russia has done is such a shame
Wish we could have had a visit to
this lovely city before
But maybe later when it is once again the same
When this nightmare ends
And peace begins

MUSIC

Ukrainians, I see them play music
and hear them sing too, in a desolate place
A young band plays songs and
raises money for their army
The girl looks so young, what a beautiful face
One Ukrainian man played the violin
in an empty field
The Ukrainians will not yield.
Also, a young man played on the piano,
John Lennon's "Imagine"
It was haunting in this setting of war
But music soothes the soul
And sometimes give hope

EASTER SUNDAY

We went to church
It was Easter Sunday
But Ukraine was on my mind
We pray for them, as we did last Sunday
And as we probably will again next Sunday-
But how many more Sundays
will we be praying for Ukraine?
I don't want it to be all in vain
I want the prayers to be answered
for these brave people in so much pain
physical and emotional,
so much pain it's hard to explain
Please God end this war soon,
make it go away we pray!
Make it go away!
Please make it go away!

BRAVE

Sometimes I go about my regular days
and no one even mentions Ukraine
how could this be?
The Ukrainian people are always on my mind
Their plight bears on my soul
So many of them are trapped in the
dark and the cold
So many children, so young, so many
Also, some are so very old
But still, they are so bold
Trapped in a world so cold
We all admire their people,
So strong and together
As a war they strive to weather

STAY THE COURSE

It's not on the front page anymore,
But on the last pages.
C'mon world pay attention
The WAR still rages!
Don't turn away
Don't leave, but stay
Stay the course
Against this evil force

ORDINARY

They were going for walks in the park
on a sunny day.
They were going to walk and going to play
Just regular life every day
The young folks were going to cafes and bars
and drinking cocktails
And now they're gathering and
making Molotov cocktails
And hoping and praying that Putin fails
They pray and fight just for their freedom back
The ordinary days we have-
They don't - their days are faded to black
I pray they can soon have their ordinary
and their peaceful days back

OVER

I've been around a long time,
and now I'm pretty old
I was a kid when the other wars unfolded
But this one is all seen in real time everyday
It's breaking my heart, like it is to so many others
Sometimes I just cry
We want it to be over.
America wants it to be over.

KEEP THEM SAFE

I never saw anything like this.
We can all see what's happening day after day.
How can we look away?
The great reporters, like Trey Yingst,
they show it to us in real time
He's back again on the front line.
His bravery is a sight to see.
He brings all the news to you and to me
we watch and see
We just want everyone to stay safe
Don't let them fall victim to this hate
Make it end before it's too late
Take care of Trey and the others,
Keep them all safe

FREEDOM AND PEACE

Now we are seeing mass graves.
But these people are so brave.
They won't back down.
They stand their ground
As war rages all around.
Some day they must have
freedom and peace

OVERCOME

Now I put pen to paper
as I wonder will it really matter?
I want to do more
I wish I could make a difference in the outcome of it all
But my efforts just seem so very small
I wish there was a way I could answer the call
a way to fight against injustice
how can we fight against the forces of evil and win?
It's like David and Goliath
but David did win, and God is on our side
against evil and for good to overcome
So, we know in spite of it all
Ukraine can win and more than overcome!

WINGS OF A DOVE

When I go to church,
I light a candle and pray for Ukraine
When I kneel by my bed to sleep,
I pray for Ukraine
When I drive to work, I pray for Ukraine
I know He hears us all as we pray for Ukraine
So many prayers sent up to above
Sent up like on the wings of a dove
All sent up out of love
So much love and thoughts and
prayers for these people
So brave and true
You must win
And let's not let this happen again

OLENA GNES

Anderson Cooper interviewed her
Did you see?
To me, she is the face of the people of Ukraine
Olena Gnes, in her eyes you see the pain
She is so very beautiful and she's a young mom
Kyiv is where's she's from
She, her husband, and kids had a nice, happy life
Now so much upheaval and strife
She and the kids had to run and hide,
Her husband had to stay and fight.

RIGHT

What's happening in Ukraine
is evil and insane.
Everyone knows who is to blame
For civilization this is a shame
When will it end?
Arm Ukraine and give their people hope
Don't give up
Stand by their people
and don't back down
And don't give up
Please people of the world,
don't let them down
Don't give up the fight
It all must turn out right!

HARVEST

Ukraine is part of the breadbasket of the world
The colors of their flag are blue and yellow
Blue is for the sky
Yellow is for the harvest
Beautiful blue sky and fields of wheat to harvest
But now there may be no harvest of wheat
No bread to bake
What will everyone eat?
Now these brave people fight to stay alive
Sometimes they have to run and hide
instead of harvest wheat, to import or eat
They'll have blue sky and a harvest again
when this war is over
This war, they must WIN!
Then they'll be the breadbasket of the world again

HEARTFELT PRAYERS

All of us, in a free world,
We worry about the people of Ukraine
How could Russia become a killing machine?
This is evil and insane
We pray every day for healing and peace
Did you see the Vatican on Easter Sunday?
Day of remarkable hope,
Thousands of people there,
At church and at home
all joined in prayers
For peace for the people of Ukraine
Heartfelt prayers to end their pain
And bring back peace to their land
People praying and holding hands

VICTORY

Victory must come for Ukraine
The world needs to see victory there!
Everyone does care
We want victory there!
Victory! Victory! Victory!
For Ukraine

TOMORROW

How could the Kremlin let this go on?
When will someone put a stop to this?
Ukrainians did not back down or run away
They had the strength and courage to stay
Zelensky meets with other leaders and takes a stand
A leader and a land both did not deserve
any of this horror
We hope and pray peace will come tomorrow!

HELP THEM

We never knew much about Ukraine
Now we love Ukraine and her people
Hope they know how much we care
We know what happened is not fair
We hope we can help them to win and
to heal in the end
We want to help them mend-
We wish all LOVE to send!

STOP

Kyiv and Lvive, cities many of us have
never heard of before
Now we know of these towns and many more
Now our hearts break for them and so many others
Their brave men and women,
and children and mothers
Mothers, Dads, babies, seniors, none are safe
All are in danger, attacked by a stranger
For no reason – no blame
It's beyond reason and an horrendous
and disastrous shame
STOP this war, and STOP it NOW
STOP this invasion, and STOP it HOW?
Listen, World, LISTEN!

EVIL

We send artillery
We send tanks
We all send prayers and love
It's innocent against evil
But we know God can defeat evil!
God can defeat evil!

POLAND CARES

Just think- what would you do if
Ukraine was your home?
What would you do?
Where would you go?
You wouldn't want to be alone.
Who would help you, anyone?
Could you run away, or try to hide and stay
Could you catch a bus or walk for miles?
Would you be okay?
It's tough to say.
Thank God for Poland,
If you could make it there
Thank God they care
Just imagine and offer up prayers
And thank God, Poland cares!

BACK

Rolling hills and pastures
Peaceful towns and cities
Picturesque scenes
This can be again.
Ukraine will be back
stronger than ever
Ukraine will be back
They'll never waiver

ENOUGH

Sanctions, Sanctions!
Doesn't seem to be enough.
Do we have someone who can be tough?
We all know Ukrainians are brave…
Who else will go?
Zelensky was offered an escape,
but he did not go
No, no, he said, "No."
He's a fighter,
Not a quitter
He and his faithful soldiers,
They fight to save their great country!
To get it back as it used to be,
Just to have Ukraine back as she used to be.

SOONER

And then we turned away-
didn't look that bad
They said, "just maneuvers,
nothing to see here"
Guess what, no reason to be sad
No, nothing here is going on bad
Well, guess what?
Maybe someone
should've acted sooner
Like, maybe the rest of the world!
Like maybe the U.N.
Like someone!
Should have
Could have
Acted Sooner

MORE

We see their faces,
we see their tears
How can we look away?
What can we do?
What can we say?
We cry, too,
But tears are not enough
We don't know what to do,
You seem so far away,
yet seem so near
And your anguish is so clear
I know your lion of a leader
has a loud roar
I hope we can pray
and help you more-
We pray to God above
To please help you more

UKRANIAN PEOPLE

I'm staying up late tonight,
kneeling by my bed,
Thoughts of Ukraine
swirling in my head
How many people now are
brought to their knees?
How many people are asking God,
"please help Ukraine even more"
God, hear the prayers of your people
Praying and worshiping at home,
displaced or under a steeple
Please, please, God answer the
prayers of your people!
For the Ukrainian people!

NEVER BE GONE

None of us know what to do
But it can't be hopeless and gone
Ukraine is too special, as we've been shown
Ukraine will never be all alone
Ukraine also, can NEVER be gone!

WHY?

So much pain
How can we go there again?
No place to hide
We feel this inside
It hurts our hearts
The world needs a new start
This war is so unjust
If there's anything we can do, we must
But what can we do?
As we sit and see and cry,
And ask, "Why? Why? Why?"

FIGHTERS

God bless Malcomb Nance,
decorated former U.S. Naval Officer
He has gone to fight for Ukraine
Some others have done the same
There's an "International
Legion for Defense of Ukraine"
About 20,000 are taking a stand
They stand and fight
For the freedom of this land!
They are HEROS for sure
They fight for a noble cause in defense
of a land under attack
But these men too will
"have Ukraine's back."

TOWNS

Now we're seeing mass graves,
but the people were so brave
They won't back down
The people, and their leader,
They stand their ground!
Although Russia and her soldiers
are pushing them around,
Burning their towns
Kharkiv, Lviv, Mariupol, Kyiv, and others,
we know your names too
We see your pain now
When will this end and how?
We hope it ends soon!
We people in America,
We "Love you to the Moon."

ED SHEERAN

I saw Ed Sheeran in Ukraine
It looked like a beautiful background,
Like a town square, very picturesque, very serene
Hope it is still a beautiful scene
Hope that town is still serene
God bless Ed Sheeran
Let his music play on day, after day, after day!
He's playing at a concert to help Ukraine
God bless Ed Sheeran again and again!

WELCOME

WE must stay strong
We can't give up hope
We want these people to get to go home
But, the ones who come here
WE want to make welcome!
For the ones who come to the U.S.A.
What can we do to take your stress away?
What can we do to help with your stay?
Whether your stay is short or long
Please feel that you Belong!

FREEDOM

We Love Red, White and Blue
But now we respect and love the
Blue and Yellow, too
Because your people seem so brave and true
We all must be patriotic and love our land,
If or when we have to take a stand
So, let's all be united in our quest
to always have freedom
Stand together and from each other learn.
Stand together in the lessons we learn from the war
Stand with each other and let freedom roar.
Always stay strong and let our freedom soar.

HE'S GONE

Now a young, handsome American fighter
was killed in Ukraine
He wanted to help like so many others
Now he's gone from his young wife and son,
The little boy's mother
He wanted so much to help,
but what a price to pay
So many others have gone there and may stay
Heart in hand and guns to carry
They must be weary
But they go, they sign up
We just pray they return safe and sound
And looking up in victory,
Recorded in history.

REFUGEE AND A NURSE

He was a refugee, and I was a nurse
How did we know where this would lead?
They brought him to the clinic because he was hurt
But he still seemed so alert.
Our eyes met and the feeling was deep.
I composed myself and asked,
"Where are you hurt?"
"In my body and soul"
I saw the blood on the sheets
and really hoped I could make his body whole.
It was shrapnel from a bomb in Lviv
Because he stayed to fight, and did not leave
And now this brave man is injured and sad
I wanted to put my arms around him and cry
But I couldn't, though I wanted to so bad.
Another nurse came and hooked up the I.V.,
then cut off his pants
And we saw all the wounds on his legs
So bad, so sad
The doctor came in and said, "take him to surgery"
And running down the hall we went
I came in early the next day
I ran straight to his room where I wanted to stay,
but there were more people to help that day
I came back at the end of my long day.
I wanted to see what he would say-

He asked me if he could see a Priest,
so I ran and found Father Dan
Then I walked home and went to bed.
The next morning, he gave a weak smile
when I came in.
I knew then this struggle, he could win.
Days and weeks of rehab went by.
I stopped to see him everyday
I could tell he was well on his way
But when he left, he came back!
We're together now and work together, too
To help all these people hurt from
the war and the gloom
Also, we'll be married soon!

ABOUT THE AUTHOR

Author, Judy Sevec was born in Pensacola, Florida. She lived between Florida and Alabama. She worked for many years as a waitress, and her love for people made her job very rewarding. She met her husband of twenty-eight years, Tony, through a dear friend. Tony is a Catholic, and she became Catholic. She and Tony reside in Dothan, Alabama. Her first book, "Random Thoughts on Life & Love," is a collection of poems that reflect everyday thoughts on the beauty of life and the memories of days gone by. She hopes that her passion for writing and for the people of Ukraine will inspire you to make a difference and get involved.

With every purchase of this book, she is donating 50% of its profit to help the people of Ukraine.

Poems For Ukraine

Poems For Ukraine